SAY YES to YES

And get your heart's desires,
again & again & again

Also by Sheila Kamuda

My Badass Journal
My Badass Gratitude Journal
The Little Book of Badass Feelings
Party of One

SAY YES to YES

And get your heart's desires,
again & again & again

Sheila Kamuda

R

Regan Press

SAY YES to YES

And get your heart's desires,
again & again & again

ISBN: 979-8-218-81776-3

R

Regan Press

For Sydney

Whose boundless curiosity,
love of possibility, and open heart
remind me to always say yes.

CONTENTS

Prologue

Can you imagine your life if simply saying YES brought you everything you desired? That's what I want for you. I want you to say yes to the most important person in your world. YOU. I want you to stop playing small and start saying yes to the Badass life you deserve. I want you to say yes and witness magic radiate from that, again and again, and again.

We've heard repeatedly how important it is to say no. We are encouraged to learn how to say no. To not be afraid of that little word.

But what about saying yes? Does that mean we give in? That we get walked on? That we become people-pleasers?

I will explain. Saying yes is an internal and external job. It means acknowledging, embracing, and accepting yourself. It also means being available for each experience that shows up in your life.

Saying yes has opened up my world and given me my heart's desires, and the 18 insights I am sharing with you, will, open yours.

These insights came after my partner passed away. I spent several years in the dark, hoping the next day would be the one I would feel better. I didn't know if that day would come. But it did, finally, when I was courageous enough to ask, what was on the other side of fear, and go there.

I changed. Was different. More confident. I started living the life I wanted and realized my only limitations were the ones I put on myself. I realized I was saying yes.

What about you? Do you stop yourself from having what you really want? Perhaps you don't think it's possible. Maybe you've even given up. It's time to stop living with limitations. It's time to start saying yes, and bring what you want to manifest, into your reality.

These ideas are a way of being. A framework. Words to rely on and refer to. Once you have them in your life, you will start to recognize the clues. Those last few pieces to the puzzle you've been searching for all your life will be found. And you will breathe a sigh of relief, and satisfaction, and joy.

Each one is easier to embody than you might imagine, and can help you make mindset shifts that you've been putting off. If you've wanted to say yes but weren't sure how to go about it, help is on the way.

I didn't know about these while I was slogging through my healing journey. I realized after that these are what I had started living; they helped me open my world, see things through a different lens, and say yes.

I've put these into 18 bite-size lessons for you, to help you get your heart's desires. There are several concepts within each lesson to help illustrate it, and prompts follow some of the lessons to help you experience the insight.

You can read the book straight through, or choose a lesson at random. You'll likely find yourself picking favorites and returning to them often. And there's a little extra bonus at the very end called "Because I Said Yes."

I am hoping this book will lovingly, firmly, unapologetically hit you over the head with the truth. You can do this. You can have it all.

Abandon fear, worry, self-doubt, and all the rest for a little while, and come with me on this magical journey of being available. Of saying yes.

Lesson One

All of You

There is no
duplicate of
YOU in the whole
wide world.
There never
has been; there
never will be.

—Lou Austin

ALL OF YOU

Even the yucky stuff.

I learned that if I'm going to be a success, I need all of me. The great stuff and crummy stuff that I've been through.

It's like cooking a beautiful meal. You need all the ingredients. It's not quite right if you leave something out.

That hard stuff, those difficult experiences, is part of what makes us the unique, original, capable, loyal, empathetic, courageous, loving humans we are. All of these rich and beautiful colors creates an amazing portrait, that is ours alone.

I don't want you to relive a childhood trauma. I just don't want you to throw any of yourself out. You are an original. Be proud of that.

No one else can be as magnificent as you. They do not have your history or experiences. They don't know how many times you've fallen down and gotten back up. That's your story and that's what gives you power. Because of this you are unlike anyone on this planet.

When I was a kid, I was a horrible student. I seriously stunk at it, except for English class, mainly due to poetry, which I enjoyed. I barely passed, but someone kept moving me from one year to the next. I hated the school I was sent to, and I don't think my family believed I would amount to much. For many years, that sense of failure was my identity.

Because of what I went through as a student, I understand that learning is not "one size fits all."

And now, I wouldn't change that awful experience for anything. It gave me two beautiful gifts: that of patience and the ability to break down and simplify concepts in many ways.

Another event in my past was when Bob, my partner, passed away. My healing journey was extremely long. And when I chose to find the courage to see what was on the other side of grief, I emerged with a new sense of me. A stronger me, an empowered me, and that is a gift born out of trauma.

But you know what? I need all of me. The embarrassments, no direction, my grief journey, love of poetry, and so much more. And I wouldn't change a thing, even for a chateau in Paris (and I love Paris.)

Accepting everything is what makes us magnificent.

Simply put, you need ALL OF YOU. You need to love all of you, embrace all of you, be proud of all of you. Say yes to all of you. Because everything has made for a richer life.

If we deny or push down part of us, we may not see the gift that is waiting for us.

And there is a gift. If we can look beyond the disappointments, setbacks, losses, and accept that these are the very hurdles that have helped us evolve into the brilliant humans we are.

Your Turn

This difficult circumstance helped me become...

_____

_____

_____

_____

_____

_____

_____

_____

Lesson Two

No Apologies

We are
already FOUND,
already truly, entirely
wildly, messily
marvelously
who we were
born to be.

—Anne Lamott

NO APOLOGIES

No, you first!

I used to be a chronic apologizer. I'd be waiting for a bus and apologize as I'd motion for someone to go in front of me. That's all well and good, but why did I apologize? It's as if the words "I'm sorry" spilled out of my mouth on cue.

How many times have I said to someone when expressing my opinion, "I'm sorry to say..." I'm not sorry to say at all. What was that about?

I can't even count how many times I've apologized for liking champagne, city walks instead of hikes, theatre, and naps in the afternoon. Or feeling awkward and apologizing because I stink at math and have a lousy sense of direction.

When we apologize, we put ourselves in the #2 position. We're hiding. Bottom line, we aren't loving ourselves (well, not enough). We might as well say, "Here, take my power." It diminishes who we are, and gives permission for others to treat us in the #2 position.

There is no way you can be open to possibilities if you're living in the space of apologizing.

In fact, you won't even see opportunities appearing right in front of you, unless you start liking who you are.

It's time for us to accept who we are, completely, fully, entirely, and realize that we are having a beautiful impact on others, just by being ourselves.

Whatever you like or dislike, are good at or not so much, you do you. Make no apologies for your YOU-NESS.

And when you do this, when you stop apologizing for you, you start validating yourself. Yes. You start believing that what you have to say is valid.

When you make a habit of apologizing, you open the door for Imposter Syndrome to come waltzing in whenever some tiny, insignificant event triggers you into believing you lack a skill, or are unqualified. It's very good at making you feel bad and needing to apologize for your seeming lack of credentials, even though you are clearly an expert.

This imposter monster is your gremlin. it wants you to play it safe by making you feel like a fake.

And if it gets its way, you'll talk yourself right out of that amazing opportunity just waiting for you.

This is no time to give in to this gremlin. You lack nothing. You are a master of your craft. The moment Imposter Monster invites itself into your head, you must show it the door and firmly say that you have no room for it in your life.

This feeling of not having the credentials triggers you to apologize for something completely untrue. Recognize this and do not keep the world from your brilliance another moment.

Something wonderful happens when you stop apologizing for who you are. You gain confidence. You stand taller. You smile more. Your self-esteem grows. You look in the mirror and like what you see.

At one time, someone's words might have ridiculed you, dismissed you, embarrassed you, made you feel small. But as if you've become a Superhero, these bullets of mockery and meanness now bounce right off.

You are untouchable. All because you are making no apologies for who you are. All because, you like you.

And with this newfound you, you become open to the world around you and more aware of all the possibilities waiting for you.

A beautiful experience you would have missed before is clearly in front of you for the taking. You don't understand how you never saw it before. And it changes your world.

Your Turn

Name five things (or more) that you like about yourself.

_____

_____

_____

_____

_____

_____

_____

Your Turn

Finish this sentence:

I will no longer apologize for...

_____

_____

_____

_____

_____

_____

_____

Lesson Three

Speak Your Truth

The privilege of
a lifetime
is BEING
who you are.

—Joseph Campbell

SPEAK YOUR TRUTH

Definitely not Cha-Cha lessons.

When I was a kid growing up in New York, every summer, my mom and dad would take my older sister and me to the Catskills for a boring two weeks at a shabby hotel. (Think one step below *Dirty Dancing* if that helps.)

There were two highlights: Cha-Cha lessons by the pool and Talent Night.

As exciting as that sounds, I remember asking my mom why we couldn't ever go somewhere like, say, Paris. (Leave it to me to always offer fancier options.)

My mom responded, as she always did when I'd ask for something that seemed too grand, "That's for RICH people." And that was my truth for many years. Until it wasn't.

The message was very clear. That's for someone else, not us.

The words "that's for rich people" hung in the air throughout my childhood, and imprisoned me into believing I couldn't have certain things. Like that prospect was impossible, not even on the table, and ridiculous to even consider. My parents lived in a state of scarcity. There was no other option.

As I got older, I decided that kind of thinking was not for me. That kind of life was not for me. I wanted to live big. And in that moment, I realized, that was my mom's truth, not mine.

I started to speak my truth.

.

And I did go to Paris, many times. And I learned that it was for anyone. All you needed to do was just believe you could. Believe it was possible. For you.

Don't be afraid to speak your truth. To be who you are and accept your heart's desires. It's okay to be an original.

You have a voice. Trust what you believe in. Make sure you're being true to your story, and not someone else's story. If you don't align, that's alright.

Always, speak your truth. (And then if you want to take Cha-Cha lessons, go for it.)

Your Turn

What is your truth?

Lesson Four

Showing Up

I am
the MASTER
of my fate.
I am
the captain
of my soul.

—William Ernest Henley

SHOWING UP

Yes, like you own the place.

We want to be liked so much. We want to be part of the group. Be invited. Not cast out. Not alone.

And we'll turn ourselves inside out hoping that someone likes us or hires us or follows us. We spend our life convincing others.

This is not the way to show up.

When you try to convince someone, you're thinking, "You are so much better than me, smarter than me, funnier than me...." And you stop being the real you for someone you're trying to impress. You want validation from a stranger. And when you put them up on a pedestal, the only direction they can look at you, is down. They will never see you as an equal.

Convincing has that awful vibe of neediness or desperation. And we all know that gets us nowhere and repels the thing (or person) we want.

We want so much to be loved. Getting wrapped up in that instead of knowing who we are and that we have a place in this big, beautiful world.

You might have done this at a job interview. Throw everything at them so they like you, and pray they hire you. And if you don't get the job, after killing yourself trying to win them over, you're left depleted and demoralized.

Same is true with friendships. We work so hard at trying to convince, instead of liking ourselves enough to just bring us.

When do we like ourselves enough to stop convincing? To stop trying so hard? To stop being a follower? To just be?

And while we're at it, enough of this "people pleasing" stuff. When you people please, you're taking care of others. You leave yourself behind. You just give and give. This is not how you want to show up.

People pleasing can be very tricky. If you practice it enough, you become expert at it. You might do it to win someone's favor — a boss, family members, a friend.

You might do it because you don't like to make waves. You consider yourself the peacekeeper, and don't want to make a big deal about it, so you do the damn thing. Again.

And this means that you aren't setting boundaries, which adds up to not choosing you. You are choosing them. They matter more than you.

This is what you've been practicing. And, when a big, wonderful, amazing opportunity comes knocking at your door, you get excited. You're up for it. You do all the things to get it.

Except for one little problem. You've not been choosing you, so when this awesomeness drops in your lap, you're not ready for it. You're not practiced at choosing you. And this miracle will slip out of your hands.

Second cousin to "people pleasing" is "enabling." We want to cheer our people on, support them, love them, be there for them, but enabling is something else entirely. When we do this, the message is "I don't think you're capable enough." "I don't believe you have the stuff." This does not help them. And this is no way for you to show up.

Like yourself enough to set boundaries. To choose you. That is one of the kindest things you can do for yourself.

Now promise me, no more hard selling. No more people pleasing. No more enabling. No more thinking someone else is better than you, no matter what their position or title or clothing label is.

Remember: If you don't value yourself, admire yourself, believe in yourself, you will attract people in your life, who don't value, admire, or believe in you.

Be excited for who you are and trust what you "bring to the party." These are your special talents, skills, and personal attributes. This is what makes you different from others. Believe it. Own it.

If the friendship, the job, or whatever else, doesn't pan out, love yourself above all else, and know there is so much better waiting for you.

Always be around people that help you show up as your best self. People that make you feel good, make you laugh, uplift you, encourage you, love you, and pull the magic out of you.

Your Turn

What do you "bring to the party"? Write a list of your talents, skills, personal attributes. This is where you toot your own horn!

Lesson Five

The World is Waiting for You

Can you remember
who you were,
BEFORE
the world told you
who you should be?

—Charles Bukowski

THE WORLD IS WAITING FOR YOU
What are you waiting for?

We have an idea, a moment of inspiration. We're working on a piece of writing, or music or art or dance or painting or any endeavor.

We're afraid to let our stuff fly. We're tentative to let it go. I get it. It's not that we don't want to send it out into the world. But we're vulnerable. We don't want to be laughed at or ignored.

So what do we do? We either curl up into a ball and stay on our comfy couch, never letting the damn thing see the light of day, or we play with it, tinker with it, edit it to death, till there's nothing left but bones.

We need to get out of our heads, and start believing that underneath the junk could be a buried treasure, waiting to be unearthed and shared with the world.

We've forgotten we are in charge. We aren't six, being told the picture of the barn we drew shouldn't be purple. We can make the barn any color we want. We are running the show. We are the boss of our creation.

The strangers who give you an opinion are not in charge. Why are we always letting people push us around? People will interpret your work as they wish, with their filters. And that's ok.

If your work is original, rest assured it will take your audience a while to get used to it, and wrap their brains around it.

You gotta hang tough.

Start caring more about what *YOU* think than about what anyone else thinks.

I'm not suggesting that opinions are meaningless. You can share ideas and stages of your work with trusted friends. They might help you see something from a different angle. And then you become even better at your craft.

And I love the sound of applause as much as the next guy, but your audience cannot be more important than you. The creator of your work.

Stop being afraid to hit the send button. Let it fly. That's how we gain confidence, get used to our critics, and trust in our creative juices.

That's how we learn and evolve. We can't do that if our endeavors only exist in our head. I've tried. There's nothing like putting an idea out there to see how we might change it the next time.

This is almost magical for me: waiting to see what I'll see once my project has "left the building."

What's the worst that could happen?

You realize that after you let it fly, a pastel pink would make your illustration pop? An upbeat refrain would add more dimension to your song? More humor in the third act of your play would add comic relief? Tilting the dancer's head up would make the choreography a little edgier? Shooting the film from a side view would give it more depth?

GOOD!

This is how we improve, develop, evolve, and emerge greater than before. Yes, that's what we're supposed to do.

If you don't hit your send button, that same inspiration will most certainly show up in someone else's genius. And you'll be kicking yourself saying, "That's what I was going to say (paint, write, compose...)."

We cannot stop inspiration when it is ready and the world needs to have it now. So it will find a way. Through you, or someone else. So, why not you?

Isn't that better, even if you feel your inspiration is not perfect, than not acting on it at all? Make that leap. You can always refine afterward.

And while we're on the subject of perfection, why must anything be perfect the first time? And who's to say what perfect is?

Let's try to abandon that stuffy idea of perfection at the first try. Or better yet, believe the first try *is* perfect. Tomorrow it will be perfect again, with new knowledge, or new inspiration.

We are a work in progress. What we create tomorrow does not diminish what we created today. And we couldn't create today without yesterday.

Celebrate it all. You are a magnificent work in progress. Be excited for each new idea you bring into the world.

Remember, the world is waiting for you. What are you waiting for?

Your Turn

What amazing inspiration has come to you?
Who will you send it to? (This is your
practice.)

Lesson Six

Shit Happens

Stop worrying
where you're going
MOVE ON.
If you can know
where you're going,
you've gone. Just
keep moving on.

—Stephen Sondheim

SHIT HAPPENS

Surrender (something better is coming).

We need to control everything. That seems to be how so many of us are wired.

It's not easy bending. We want what we want. And that is to control the outcome. We sometimes even want to control the outcome for others.

The more we try to control, the more it slips through our fingers. If we could just trust, instead of forcing the outcome, everything would be so much better, easier, smoother.

There is a reason a situation has entered your life. The reason you were told "no" doesn't make sense at the time, and can make you quite bitter and angry. Yes, shit happens.

But when given some space—and it may take some time—that wretched disappointment does fall into place. Something we didn't know about, was necessary. Something we needed was vital to our growth. And the outcome is always so much better and brilliant.

In fact, our lives can become so much richer, so much more rewarding, because that letdown, which we thought was so unfair, and thoughtless, and stupid, caused us to find a different road. The road we're actually supposed to be on, but would have never chosen.

Call this divine intervention or coincidence, but there have been some enormous rejections throughout my life that forced me to think more broadly. And I would never have done that without the setbacks.

By needing to think of a plan B, to figure out what I would do, since someone put the brakes on my plan A, my entire world expanded. Even when I think about this now, it blows my mind.

If the decision-makers had agreed with my idea, my road would have been easy, and I would NEVER have the success I do. My brain would have been on autopilot. I wouldn't have had to figure out another way.

The new plan took time, but once I was on a roll, that momentum was incredible. And it led me to ventures I would not have thought possible. Products I would never have fathomed. Expansion of my original desire that opened new worlds. And I let the outcome be. I didn't try to wrangle it. I let all of it lead me.

Once you take an action, let it be. Let it go. Surrender. Do not worry about it. Do not harp on it. Do not obsess over it. Do not try to control it.

Just give it space. Things need space. We can't just take an action and expect the results in five minutes. This is important. It is a seed in the ground. Just water it, and stop trying to dig it up to see how it's doing.

Learn to bend. Don't hold on so tight to it. If the outcome is not what you expected, stomp around for five minutes spitting fire, and then know that the right help, friends, job, situation, is coming. Because the Universe has a much better plan for you than you could have ever imagined.

Act on It. Believe it. Own it. Let it go.

Lesson Seven

You Get to Choose

Your GIFTS
matter.
Your STORY
matters.
Your DREAMS
matter.

—Michael Oher

YOU GET TO CHOOSE

I'm the big cheese in my life?

I learned that a quick temper and sarcasm will only get you so far. I spent many years hiding behind both, and finally decided to choose another way to show up.

It's an amazing thing, realizing we can choose everything. How we want to feel. How we want to respond. How we want to face the day. How we want to live.

If we don't like our script, we can change it. We are our own playwrights. We can rewrite every scene in our lives. I used to think everything was set in stone. But rewriting changes the trajectory of our life. We write the pages of our life, and rewrite as necessary.

When we choose, we take 100% responsibility for our actions. We're in charge.

We also choose when we decide to live intentionally. That means taking the time to think about what you want each day, and as you move through your day. To not just float along being pushed and pulled around by circumstances.

Setting an intention means "on purpose" and "with purpose." If you want to take a walk, listen to music, eat ice cream, cook a meal, have coffee with a friend, volunteer, go shoe shopping, plan a trip...do it intentionally.

When I'm living with Intention, everything is always better. I feel less anxious. More accomplished. My energy is better. I have direction.

And the best part is, I've chosen this. I've given this gift to myself. Being intentional is one of those little gems that, if added to your everyday life, will magically make things easier.

The next time you feel you don't have control over your life, give yourself some space, breathe, and choose. Don't just drift around letting others make choices for your life.

Think about what mood you will choose when you wake up tomorrow. And the day after. And the day after that.

Choose to do things that help you feel good. Choose to be kind to yourself. Choose to be generous. Choose to be grateful. Choose to celebrate, even small wins. And choose yourself first. This is self-love.

Your Turn

What event in your life would you rewrite? (Make it good. You are the playwright of your life.)

_____

_____

_____

_____

_____

_____

_____

_____

Lesson Eight

You Have Power

You have
WITHIN you
all wisdom,
all power,
all strength,
all understanding.

—Eileen Caddy

YOU HAVE POWER
Lightsaber not required.

Power isn't only reserved for those with clout. Power isn't a special privilege for the super smart, super rich, or super strong.

That word "power" looms over us. It's a loud word. People in charge make us cower, or they have celebrity status so we put them high up on a pedestal.

We don't think we have any power so that's how we live. It becomes one of those terrible patterns we've done to ourselves, and we must stop.

We are more powerful than we realize. We can create our world. We just have to start believing that. Think about Dorothy (*Wizard of Oz*) and the ruby slippers. She had the power to go home all along, but didn't realize she could access it. We can access our power. We just need to believe we can.

We are powerful humans having an impact on our world. That's daunting, I know. That we are actually creating what we are living. And it starts with our thoughts. Always remember: What you think about, you bring about.

Everything in our life is what we've been practicing. So if we want a different result, we must have a different practice.

The power to create the life we want is within. If we want to change a lifelong behavior, we can. If we want to change how we respond, we can. If we want to change our beliefs of fear and lack to love and generosity, we can. If we want to change our complaining to thoughts of gratitude, we can

There is also power in how we talk to ourselves. If you don't think you are creating your world by the words you say day in and day out, think again.

The next time you talk down to yourself, do a rewrite. You'll be amazed that this negative self-talk has become your constant companion. We beat ourselves up and then wonder why we don't have a good self-image. Words have power, and you are in charge of your words.

Negative talk keeps us small. It may feel good while we're doing it, but a terrible aftertaste remains. We don't need that to be part of our life anymore.

Believe you have the power to create what you want. To feel confident in that belief. To be clear about what you want. And to feel worthy of your heart's desires.

Your Turn

What would you like to change?
What will you no longer be available for?
What new practice will you implement?

Your Turn

What loving words will you say to yourself?
Let these become your constant
companion.

_____

_____

_____

_____

_____

_____

_____

_____

Lesson Nine

Exactly Where You Should Be

I wish you could
see yourself
through my eyes.
Then you would
know just how
AMAZNG

you are.

—Katrina Mayer

EXACTLY WHERE YOU SHOULD BE

Where is that again?

There is a feeling of angst about not moving fast enough. Have you felt that? Like we're always playing catch-up. It doesn't help when we look around us and start doing the "comparing" dance. Then we start feeling worthless, and don't think we'll ever make it. Like a never-ending audition.

We don't want to believe we are exactly where we should be. That sounds so hum-drum. So defeating. So not sexy.

We don't like realizing that there are steps we need to take, to make our craft better, and to make us better. There's nothing worse than being on stage and not being ready. This is what this time is for.

And if you think the next guy is having success faster, it's doubtful. But even if they are, they have their path. You have yours.

The real question is, Why aren't you looking back to see how far you've come? Because, I am sure, you have had many twists and turns. Don't take this for granted. Realize the events that are happening are perfect for you now. Are exactly what you need.

It's necessary to keep adding the right ingredients that make up the deliciousness you are. Your destination will be that much sweeter if you give yourself time to simmer.

Feel the joy in becoming the amazing human you are meant to be. Find delight in the lessons. Then shine for the world.

We don't like the uncertainty of it all. We want to know exactly when the success is going to happen and how long it will take. (And we don't like waiting.)

I know you don't want to hear this, but we must trust the process. We must follow every breadcrumb. These come in many ways. From a friend, a song lyric, a book, a movie, a road sign, and on and on. These little clues are like buried treasures.

Be open to the gathering of information. It is so much better than rushing the journey. Be patient. Take the winding road, with beautiful waterfalls, and mountains, and wildflowers along your way.

If you compare your Now Self to your last week's self or last year's self, I am certain you will be happily surprised by your immense progress.

That job you now have, you would not have been ready for last year. Same is true for that relationship, career change, big move, or huge creative success.

As you look back, do you see that you are more equipped now, more mature now, more skilled now, more ready now for what life is bringing you?

Everything has a time. This is your chance to trust who you are now (and love yourself for it), and who you are becoming.

And for heaven's sake, celebrate!

Your Turn

Write a list of your wins. Nothing is too small. Remember, *YOU* have created all of this! This is your "success" list. Read it often. Out loud.

Your Turn

What adjectives describe you? Here
are a few, to start you off:
Confident. Talented. Beautiful. Fierce.
Loyal. Empathetic. Enthusiastic....

Choose what best describes you and add
the words "I am" before each.
Make these your daily affirmations.

Lesson Ten

Enough

It takes
COURAGE
to grow up
and become
who you
really are.

—e.e. cummings

ENOUGH

'Nuf said.

We are enough just as we are. Without having to do anything or be anything or prove anything.

We are enough because we exist. We breathe. We are here.

Now this may be hard to grasp because all our life it's been: "Did you land the job?" "Did you plan the trip?," "Did you finish the novel?" "Did you buy the car?" "Did you get engaged?"

It's all about what we've accomplished, not who we are. We've heard this since we were kids. So everything has been based on our achievements. Victories are wonderful, but we are enough without them.

Practicing the belief that we are enough needs to be a priority. That, and loving who we are right now. Not when...

Not when your book hits the bestseller list. Not when someone tells you you're beautiful. Not when your song is #1. Not when you become CEO. Not when you win an Oscar. Not when you buy your first home. Not when you quit your job and build your business.

Not when you get to wherever you think you need to be. You are enough, now. (That other shiny stuff is just the icing on the cake.)

Your Turn

Write down the words "I am enough right now."

What do these words mean to you?

_____

_____

_____

_____

_____

_____

Lesson Eleven

Follow Your Gut, Not Your Gremlin

Don't look at
your feet
to see
if you are
doing it right.

JUST DANCE.

—Anne Lamott

FOLLOW YOUR GUT, NOT YOUR GREMLIN

That's your Hell Yes.

Your gremlin (saboteur, demon, inner critic) is there to protect you. That is its whole job. And it thinks of nothing else.

But your gut, your intuition, is your built-in guidance system. And it knows what's up. Always.

Your gut is your true self. When you follow it, everything is calmer, better, seamless. You are in flow.

Your gut knows the things you really want. These things energize you. Even if they're scary, and maybe more than you think you can handle.

Your gremlin will do everything in its power to keep you safe. So you don't do anything, change anything, try anything.

When your gremlin whispers to you "don't do it," making you feel frightened and powerless, STOP. Recognize this is Mr. Gremlin. Understand that it will never leave you alone because it loves you. It doesn't know that you aren't five anymore, and do not need its protection.

The more you recognize this gremlin, the less power it will have over you, and the stronger you will become. So ignore it, or tell it to get lost. Yes, again. I often tell my gremlin to just go get a cocktail somewhere and leave me alone.

Know that your gut will always guide you. Always lead you on your path. It will take you from one simple idea to another.

Like breadcrumbs. Follow them. This is key to having everything you want. Everything you dream about.

My gut led me to having my wedding at the Rainbow Room, even though Bob, my partner, almost fainted when I excitedly suggested it.

"Rockefeller Center Rainbow Room?" *Yup, THAT ONE.*

We had gone there on several special occasions, danced on their revolving floor, and had scrumptious dinners. And, I knew they had suites for private functions.

We planned on a small guest list. Help came in the form of a menu we could manage, tips from a friend on affordable flowers that were stunning, live music that was reasonable.

Little things like that came to our rescue. I followed my gut and ended up with an unforgettable, beautiful, black tie, intimate wedding at the Rainbow Room.

♡

Another time, I had a yearning to travel to Paris. This was five years after Bob died. We had been there several times before, so it wasn't totally unfamiliar.

I was finally ready to make this huge leap on my own. I was scared shitless, but so excited at the thought of it.

I did it. I stayed in the 5th arrondissement, bustling with young people, right near the bookstore Shakespeare and Company and diagonal from Notre Dame.

I'll never forget that I traveled to Paris. On my own. I followed my gut. It was a lovely adventure, and an important part of my growth journey.

To follow your gut means to trust yourself, your ideas, what's lurking inside you, and show up.

Show up every day as the person you want to share with the world. This is where you don't look around to others to see if you're doing it right. How the hell can someone else, know if *YOU* are doing it right?

But, if you need a hero to get you started, who do you look up to? Who has the kind of courage you want to emulate? Who brings it every day without caring if others are hopping on board? That's your hero. Someone who's the real deal. Someone who's putting their heart and soul into their passion.

They don't question, "Do I do this now? Do I go here? Take it this far?" They don't need validation. They just do the damn thing.

They feel it and follow their gut. And they don't care who comes along. (Usually, everyone does.) The great ones never care. They just believe in themselves.

Your power is in following your gut, your intuition. If you aren't sure whether you're being led by your gut or your gremlin, ask yourself if you're excited, even if it scares you. Now, your gremlin will try to hold you back with scare tactics to protect you. But if you're elated, and I mean a Hell Yes kind of enthusiasm that will not go away, it's your gut. Follow it.

It's either a Hell Yes or a Hell No. There is no Hell Maybe.

.

Your Turn

Write a short letter to your gremlin telling it
to get lost. Remember to give your gremlin
a name.

Your Turn

Who's your hero? Who shows up every day,
pulling out all the stops? What excites you
about this person?

Lesson Twelve

Be Available

Dare to live
the life
you have
DREAMED
for yourself.

Ralph Waldo Emerson

BE AVAILABLE
You mean, always?

Why is it so hard to be available? For all opportunities. Great ones and tough ones.

The great ones give us chances. This is the universe saying "I got you." I know what you want. Here's your next clue. Take it.

These will keep tapping us on the shoulder. Begging us to follow. We sometimes miss them. Especially if they're too small, we might ignore them. They may not be glamorous enough, so we aren't available for them. We might even trip over these beautiful opportunities, trying to find something bigger. More seductive.

The hard ones are there to teach. These are the lessons. To help us evolve. Become the success, the leader, the star, the one, the trailblazer.

And they may come in the form of disappointments. These are the ones that make you want to throw in the towel. You may even believe this is a sign to give up on your dreams. But given enough time, these very circumstances will be the catalyst to incredible creativity, and joy, and success that you were not even aware was coming.

The Universe always gives you what you need. And that invariably leads you to exactly what you wanted, only in technicolor!

I can think of several hugely disappointing situations in my life. I was quite angry and disillusioned. Life would have been so easy. If only...

Years later, I realized that difficulty made my life richer and more complete than if I had gotten my way. I had needed obstacles. I had needed to not take the lazy way out. I had needed to know what I could do. What I was capable of.

When you do take the opportunity, don't rush through it. Watch how it opens up before you. Savor every moment. And be grateful.

If you were dining at a five-star restaurant, you would take time to dress, excited about the lovely dinner ahead.

Once at the restaurant, you might order a cocktail. Sip it. Make conversation with your companion. Linger. Look at the gorgeous surroundings.

Maybe it is the most exquisite restaurant you've seen. You would take your time. You wouldn't want it to end. You would appreciate each moment.

The meal is supposed to be long, luxurious, special. The point is not to get to the end and pay the bill. But to enjoy and relish each moment, each delicious morsel.

The Universe wants you to think of everything in your life as a five-star experience. To not just think of the end and figure out how fast you can get to it.

Luxuriate in it. Take time. Be present. Look around. Indulge. Live in each magical moment. Celebrate it. Be available to the possibilities. And to each opportunity.

Let the Universe tap you on the shoulder. Be aware. Be awake. Don't drift through your life. It's all for you. Start to see it. Start to practice saying yes. Start to recognize the clues. The breadcrumbs.

I keep mentioning breadcrumbs and this may conjure up visions of fairytales. However, if you can put that aside, each breadcrumb is your guide.

One breadcrumb will lead to another, and an epiphany or the simple answer you've been searching for will appear.

A friend was in town for a short visit and asked if we could get together. She and another friend of hers were planning to go to the theatre. She had an extra ticket and asked if I'd like to go.

Yes, I wanted to see her (breadcrumb), and yes, I wanted to see the play (breadcrumb). It was great fun, and after the theatre, we all went back to this friend's place to hang a bit before dinner at a restaurant I had not been to before (breadcrumb).

Her apartment was stunning, and I was admiring her bathroom tiles. We started to chat, and she told me who she had hired and mentioned a plumber (breadcrumb) and other great finds. I was in desparate need of a plumber. I could not find any that could fix a mammoth problem. Until that moment.

All of this because I was available. If I hadn't said yes to mooting up with my friend, I wouldn't have enjoyed her lovely company. I wouldn't have gone to a play I wanted to see. I wouldn't have enjoyed a scrumptious meal with wonderful people, in a new restaurant.

I wouldn't have learned about a skilled plumber who fixed a critical and extremely frustrating problem that had baffled several others.

All breadcrumbs.

Some were tiny breadcrumbs, nothing you would think would make any difference at all.

Being available moves us closer and closer to our dreams. To what our true self wants. This is what we've been asking for. What we've been wanting. This is how we get there.

Your Turn

Describe a situation for which you were
available. How did it impact your life?

Your Turn

The next time you take a walk, do not rush.
Notice beautiful things around you. Write
about what you saw and how you felt.

Lesson Thirteen

Stop Settling

I'm going to
make everything
around me
BEAUTIFUL.
That will be
my life.

—Elsie de Wolfe

STOP SETTLING
Wait for it...

That word "settle" makes me cringe.

Why do we settle? We settle for the job, the apartment, the relationship. We get duped into thinking that what we want will never come. We're impatient. We don't think that what we want is possible, or that we have what it takes to have our heart's desire, so we settle for second best.

I remember when I was looking at condos, I almost talked myself into one, and then almost another. They were okay and had some of my "must haves," but neither was *THE* one.

I wasn't sure I was going to find the one that would make me happy, and I almost settled. But something inside me (my gut) said "don't settle."

I'm so glad I didn't. My condo was waiting for me. The one I chose was in the neighborhood I had always dreamed about living in.

Now, let me preface this by saying, it's okay to take the job as a stepping stone. It's fine to take the apartment to see how that studio in that neighborhood would work out. These things are all part of your growth.

The key is to know that. That this is just a step. This job is that stepping stone, and will lead you to the better one you've been dreaming about. And when it comes, you'll be ready for it. That is not settling.

Settling is the feeling that you cannot do better, or the right person won't come along, and maybe there is no right person for you, or the career doesn't exist.

We've all been there. It's so easy to do. To fall back into that pattern. And that is a mindset we need to ditch.

It takes believing and trusting that we can have what we want. And there's a reason for the timing, that the job or the apartment, or the person has not come into your life yet.

It may take time, which is the part we don't like. But that's when you want to assess why it's okay that you haven't gotten what you wanted, yet. Maybe this is a little test to see if you will settle or know you deserve better.

I know this isn't easy. You want what you want. And you want it now. However, you will see that the condo, the marriage proposal, the career, the travel—everything you want—has divine timing. And always works out for you.

106

Lesson Fourteen

Live Big

To see a WORLD
in a grain of sand
and a heaven in
a wild flower.
Hold infinity in
the palm of your
hand and eternity
in an hour.

—William Blake

LIVE BIG

This is where you get to have a castle.

It's okay to live big. Just needed to put that out there.

Is that a daunting prospect? To believe you can have the dream house, or the travel, or the perfect relationship, or a new career, or fame?

We had dreams when we were kids and made up stories of being kings and queens and living in a castle. (Or if you were like me, you dreamed of wearing an elegant black dress, and large sunglasses, with your hair done up in a French twist, window-shopping at Tiffany's.)

Our folks didn't want us to be disappointed about life letting us down, so they made us think practically and forget about all those fantasies.

We grew up thinking we couldn't really have our dreams. As a by-product, we learned how to think small.

We can perpetuate this scarcity mindset, and not believe we can do, have, be. Or we can bring our dreams into reality.

Okay, so maybe we won't become a queen or king or live in a castle. But if we remember that living big is a mindset, that is how we start. That is what leads us down the "live big" path, rather than the "think small" path.

When you're having doubts and think it will never be, it's time to imagine. It's time to rewrite your story.

Don't let small thinking rob you. This isn't the time for fear and feelings of lack to get a hold of you.

If we take it step by step, everything becomes easier, doable. I ask you to take one small step towards your goal every day.

Just go slow. Be intentional about what you want each day. That is the path to living big.

Living big is about not putting limitations on yourself. It is believing that you get to have what you want. Thinking small takes little effort. Thinking small is safe. It's what allows us to blame and give a hundred reasons why we can't do, have, or be.

Things like, we don't have the money, didn't get the promotion, a relationship failed, no one will water our plants—anything we can grab to keep us where we are, instead of taking action. Instead of trying to make it happen.

The perspective must be: "No one is stopping me. I was born to do this, have this, be this. I don't care if it isn't easy. This is mine. I get to have this."

We don't know when the dream will come true. But once you start living big, you cannot go back. No bump in the road, small or big, will deter you. You trust it will happen. There is no doubt.

You've come too far. You now know how to be available to opportunities. You know how to follow the breadcrumbs, and you know something wonderful, and magical, beyond your wildest dreams, is possible.

You start to get what you want because you believe you can. You believe you are worthy to have your desires. It might be small things at first. Notice these. Be grateful. Celebrate them. This momentum will lead to more.

Your Turn

What were your dreams when you were young?

Lesson Fifteen

Reframe

In order to
KICK ASS
you must first
lift up
your foot.

—Jen Sincero

REFRAME

I shouldn't do the same thing over & over?

You know the feeling when you're banging your head against the wall, doing the same thing, trying to get your business or creative endeavor flying?

And you sit there wondering why the hell nothing is happening. Or things are happening at a snail's pace.

And it's not feeling very good. The excitement is starting to wane. But you're not sure where the answers lie.

This is the time you want to remember that you are a magnificent being, with multiple talents and skills. You are not just this side of your business. It's time to reframe. That means stop doing the same thing day in and day out.

Refocus your attention on one of the other hundred things that make you, you.

When you're in this space, know that there are so many ways to nourish your soul and your creative expression. Think about what you might turn your focus to and forget— yes, forget—the other stuff for now. Immerse yourself in something else. Take a bike ride, bake, knit, sing, dance, write, draw, move your furniture around.

Put aside the stuff that is making you feel worn out from trying so hard. Put your focus on another side of you. I am sure when you come back to the business of your business, you will feel refreshed and renewed. You will be able to reimagine everything differently. Magic will happen.

I don't even think about it anymore. When one part of my business is in the waiting stage, and I feel the need to take an action, I might turn to writing. It could be a piece for my blog or my next book. I explore podcasts I'd like to appear on. I refine my website. I take a walk. I put on my favorite musical and sing at the top of my lungs. I go out for a delicious bite. I work on an idea for a new workshop. I list my successes.

I'm just saying that you have more going on than you realize. And when you turn your attention to other things that inspire you, it helps the momentum, and overall success.

Lesson Sixteen

Feeling Good

HAPPINESS
is a direction,
not a place.

—Sydney J. Harris

FEELING GOOD

What's so bad about feeling good?

Why don't we want to feel good? What are we so afraid of? There is a feeling that sooner or later the shit will hit the fan, so best not feel good. And then we won't be disappointed. We'll be ready. No surprises.

And we actually *LIKE* living this way? It's no wonder we're depleted, angry, drained, scared.

I am here to tell you this is not the way it's supposed to be. And all I can ask is that you try something different. If you don't like this new magical, mystery tour, you can go back to the safer, predictable life you've known for so long.

My guess is that once you get on board with feeling good, and believing it's ok to feel good, you'll never go back again.

This will take practice, this waking up every day and wanting to feel good. Actually living your life as if you are meant to have good things. Telling yourself you get to have this. You get to live a good life. You get to have wins.

This does not mean you won't have to reframe. You will. That's part of the magic. Learning how to navigate this beautiful, messy, journey. Being present every moment. And enjoying the doing of it.

Feeling good is not living in fake positivity. It's about choosing to believe things can be ok, instead of living each chapter of your life waiting for the next disaster.

It will take some practice, and you might have to stop watching the news. But it can be done.

The key here is to stop searching for the bad. Stop being comfortable in that anxiety. Granted, you won't have things to grumble about, but I guess that's the price for feeling good.

If you're not sure what could possibly make you feel good in this cruel, harsh world, here's some of mine, and they aren't all ginormous events: A good cup of coffee. A sunset. My cats purring. Talking to my kid. Going to a museum. Seeing some great theatre. Traveling to Paris. Taking a walk. Dancing in my living room. Eating out. Washing dishes. Window shopping.

What about you?

Your Turn

Write a list of all the things that make you feel good.

Lesson Seventeen

Reflections

Your HEART
knows
the way.
RUN in that
direction.

—Rumi

REFLECTIONS

Right back at ya.

Did you know that whatever energy, vibe, electricity, you put out, that same energy will come back to you?

Sounds like a simple concept, but damn hard for some of us to apply.

If you are worried, angry, frustrated, bitter, sad, disillusioned, complaining, fearful, that is what will be reflected back to you.

Ask yourself: "How do I treat myself?" "Am I kind?" "Am I generous?" "Am I grateful?" Remember, the Universe is your mirror. So you must treat yourself with goodness first.

When you activate kind feelings, generous feelings, grateful feelings toward yourself, the Universe cannot not deliver the same to you.

130

And if you want the world (your friends, partner, boss, colleagues, grocery clerk...) to treat you as if you're special, YOU need to treat yourself like that first. So start thinking of yourself as the beautiful human you are, as the main character in your life, and then, the Universe will say, "Oh, you like that!" and it will give you more of the same.

Live in the space of a kind heart, a generous heart, a grateful heart, for yourself and others. You will get back what you put out, only the gifts you receive will be considerably bigger than you could have imagined.

Being grateful means you are saying thank you for something you've already received. Keep doing this. The Universe will hand you more amazing opportunities to be thankful for.

Your Turn

List five things and five people, you are grateful for.

_____

_____

_____

_____

_____

_____

_____

_____

Lesson Eighteen

Shine On

Shine your light
so BRIGHT
that you
may never go
back into the
darkness.

—Celeste Cav

SHINE ON

Like the moon & the stars & the sun.

No one can be as brilliant as you. You are an amazing human who can have your heart's desires. You must believe that you are worthy to have it all. To have what you dream about.

No circumstance can diminish who you are. It doesn't matter if you don't (yet) see the success you desire, or the greatness waiting for you. Nothing can devalue you or dismiss you. Nothing can keep you from everything you want.

You shine no matter what. The greater you love yourself, the brighter you shine. No one and no circumstance can stop your brilliance.

You will have moments when you doubt. There will be events that try to pull you off your path. Small-minded people may not cheer you on. Much of the time will seem like you are waiting for the good to happen.

But it will happen.

You are the stars. Nothing can dim your light. Nothing can quiet the stirring in your soul. Nothing can keep you from your heart's desires.

Just say yes to yes.

Epilogue

When we say yes, we go on a magic carpet ride. Sometimes it's a straight path. Sometimes it zigzags or turns upside down. And sometimes, there's an unexpected detour.

When we say yes, gifts show up that help lead us to where we want to be. These gifts are clues in the form of a person just saying the right words, a book, a movie, a song lyric, our own intuition. Just about anything.

When we say yes, we learn lessons, sometimes hard ones, but always necessary. Things that will help us become our true self.

When we say yes, we remain open. We are ready for inspiration. Eager for it.

We get used to these gifts and start to look for them. We start enjoying what we are doing instead of looking for the outcome, the big payoff. We start loving our work and our life. We find joy in the doing.

We begin to love this new pattern that has become our life. We do whatever we can to receive, because we know how fulfilling it will be.

We look for the breadcrumbs. We start to be excited, like a child on their birthday.

And we remember to take the time to just be, to enjoy, to look around us. To be in awe of the beautiful things in our life. We might listen to music, dance in our living room, or let our cats purr on our bare feet and be lulled into stillness.

You will start to think about events in your life that turned out really well, because you said yes. I'll bet you can think of many times in your life that incredible, maybe even magical, experiences occurred just because you said yes.

At the end of this book, you will have a chance to write down these wondrous happenings on the pages entitled, "Because I said yes."

One last thought: These lessons come from a place of strength. It is from a place of strength, that you want to say yes. That means doing things for your highest good, loving yourself unconditionally, and knowing you matter. Always come from this place and your life will be so much richer when you do say yes.

Acknowledgements

I want to acknowledge everyone who has ever said yes. That is a courageous act, and one that should be celebrated.

Thanks to Ruth Austin for steering me towards the final title, and Carrie Urbanic for her editing skill, thoughtful suggestions, and care throughout the editing process.

About the Author

Sheila Kamuda is an empowerment coach, founder of Live Out Loud Coaching, speaker, and author of *Party of One*, *My Badass Journal*, *My Badass Gratitude Journal*, and *The Little Book of Badass Feelings*.

This book is written for everyone who wants to say yes to their dreams, but isn't sure if it's the right thing, isn't sure how to, isn't sure how saying yes can help.

Sheila hopes these words are encouraging, and inspire you to follow every opportunity that is shown to you.

Website: https://www.liveoutloudcoaching.com/
Instagram: @liveoutloudcoach
Substack: SheilaKamuda.Substack.com

Because I Said Yes...

_____

_____

_____

_____

_____

_____

_____

_____

_____

Because I Said Yes...

_____

_____

_____

_____

_____

_____

_____

_____

_____

_____

145

www.ingramcontent.com/pod-product-compliance
Lightning Source LLC
Chambersburg PA
CBHW061801120626
46550CB00005B/2085